Alphonse Mucha
Make Your Own Art Masterpiece

Publisher and Creative Director: Nick Wells
Art Director: Mike Spender
Editorial: Laura Bulbeck, Josie Mitchell
Illustrator: David Jones
Colours: Jane Ashley

FLAME TREE PUBLISHING
6 Melbray Mews
Fulham, London SW6 3NS
United Kingdom

www.flametreepublishing.com

First published 2016

18 20 21 19 17
3 5 7 9 10 8 6 4 2

All images in this book are based on the works of Alphonse Mucha (1860–1939)

A CIP record for this book is available from the British Library upon request.

ISBN 978-1-78664-046-8

Printed in China

ALPHONSE MUCHA

Make Your Own Art Masterpiece

Illustrated by David Jones

Selected by Daisy Seal

FLAME TREE
PUBLISHING

Here are some of the hues used in this book. Use these as a starting point for your own art masterpieces.

Alphonse Mucha

- **Born:** 1860 Ivanice, Moravia • **Died:** 1939 • **Movement:** Art Nouveau

Although Alphonse Mucha has been described as the quintessential Art Nouveau artist he rejected the notion. He believed that he produced art in his own way, without being part of a trend or fashion. His images are, nevertheless, iconic and readily associated with the New Art at the fin-de-siècle. Mucha's influences were drawn from a wide pool: Japanese woodcuts with blocks of bright colour were particularly common at the time and were an inspiration for many contemporary graphic artists. Being from Eastern Europe, it is not surprising that Mucha had been exposed to a wide variety of symbolic and decorative art, such as Byzantine and Moorish art, nor that he used these in his illustrations. As his work matured Mucha combined geometric images, particularly circles, with his more fluid and sinuous arabesques. His designs were always stunning with high-visual impact, displaying control, rhythm and freedom of form.

Many of Mucha's illustrations for posters featured strong central figures of young women. They are usually highly stylized, with perfect skin, nymph-like bodies and extraordinarily long tresses that more closely resemble the tendrils of a plant than real hair.

~ə~

The Arts: Painting, 1898

Colour lithograph, 60 x 38 cm (23 ⅝ x 15 in),
decorative panel

Documents décoratifs, plate 38, 1902

Colour lithograph, 46 x 33 cm (18 x 13 in),
decorative design

Moët & Chandon: Dry Impérial, 1899

Colour lithograph, 60 x 20 cm (23⅝ x 7⅞ in),
commercial poster

La Trappistine, 1897

Colour lithograph, 201 x 70 cm (79 x 27½ in),
commercial poster

Lance Parfum Rodo, 1896

Colour lithograph, 44.5 x 32 cm (17½ x 12½ in),
commercial poster

The Seasons: Autumn, 1900

Colour lithograph, 70 x 29.5 cm (27½ x 11⅝ in),
decorative panel

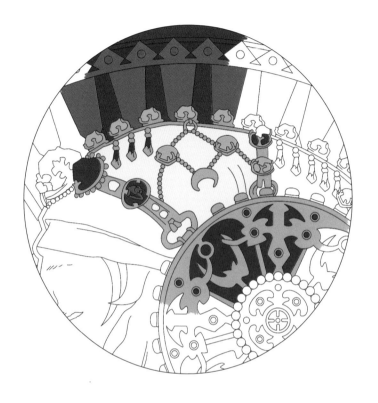

Têtes Byzantines: Blonde, 1897

Colour lithograph, 34.5 x 28 cm (13½ x 11 in),
decorative panel

Alphonse Mucha
MAKE YOUR OWN ART MASTERPIECE

Têtes Byzantines: Brunette, 1897

Colour lithograph, 34.5 x 28 cm (13½ x 11 in),
decorative panel

The Seasons: Spring, 1896

Colour lithograph, 28 x 14.5 cm (11 x 5¾ in),
decorative panel

Alphonse Mucha

MAKE YOUR OWN ART MASTERPIECE

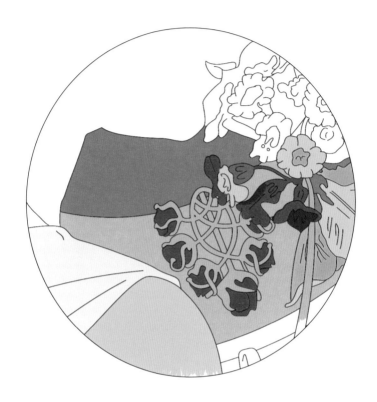

Cowslip, 1899

Colour lithograph, 71 x 27.5 cm (28 x 10⅞ in),
decorative panel

Moët & Chandon:
Champagne White Star, 1899

Colour lithograph, 60 x 20 cm (23⁵⁄₈ x 7⁷⁄₈ in),
commercial poster

The Seasons: Spring, 1900

Colour lithograph, 70 x 29.5 cm (27½ x 11⅝ in),
decorative panel

Alphonse Mucha

MAKE YOUR OWN ART MASTERPIECE

Princess Hyacinth, 1911

Colour lithograph, 125.5 x 83.5 cm (49²⁄₅ x 33 in),
theatre poster

Alphonse Mucha

MAKE YOUR OWN ART MASTERPIECE

The Seasons: Winter, 1900

Colour lithograph, 70 x 29.5 cm (27½ x 11⅝ in),
decorative panel

Alphonse Mucha

MAKE YOUR OWN ART MASTERPIECE

Heather from Coastal Cliffs, 1902

Colour lithograph, 74 x 35 cm (29 x 13¾ in),
decorative panel

Illustration based on Alphonse Mucha's

The Seasons: Autumn, 1897

Colour lithograph, 43 x 15 cm (17 x 6 in),
decorative panel

Alphonse Mucha

MAKE YOUR OWN ART MASTERPIECE

Fruit, 1897

Colour lithograph, 66.2 x 44.4 cm (26 x 17⅜ in),
decorative panel

Flowers, 1897

Colour lithograph, 66.2 x 44.4 cm (26 x 17⅜ in),
decorative panel

The Flowers: Rose, 1898

Colour lithograph, 103.5 x 43.3 cm (40¾ x 17 in),
decorative panel

The Arts: Dance, 1898

Colour lithograph, 60 x 38 cm (23⅝ x 15 in),
decorative panel

Woman with Poppies, 1898

Colour lithograph, 63.5 x 45 cm (25 x 17¾ in),
decorative panel

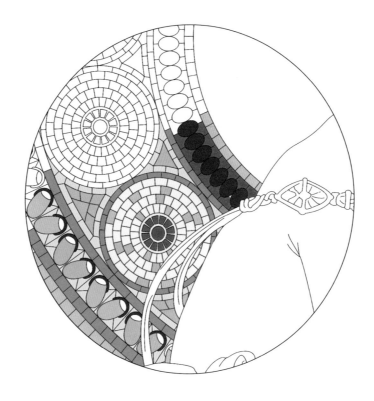

The Precious Stones: Topaz, 1900

Colour lithograph, 67.2 x 30 cm (26⅜ x 11⅞ in),
decorative panel

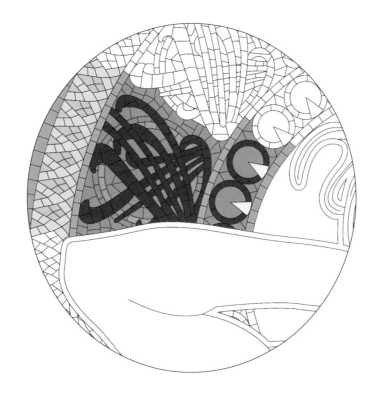

The Precious Stones: Amethyst, 1900

Colour lithograph, 67.2 x 30 cm (26⅜ x 11⅞ in),
decorative panel

Thistle from the Sands, 1902

Colour lithograph, 74 x 35 cm (29 x 13¾ in),

decorative panel

La Dame aux Camélias, 1896

Colour lithograph, 207.3 x 76.2 cm (81⅝ x 30 in),
theatre poster

Sarah Bernhardt: La Plume, 1896

Colour lithograph, 66.6 x 48.5 cm (26⅛ x 19 in),
theatre poster

Société Populaire des Beaux-Arts, 1897

Colour lithograph, 58 x 42 cm (22⅞ x 16½ in),
exhibition poster

Alphonse Mucha
MAKE YOUR OWN ART MASTERPIECE

Bières de la Meuse, 1897

Colour lithograph, 141 x 90 cm (55½ x 35⅜ in),
commercial poster

Paris International Exhibition
Decorative Plate, 1897

Ceramic, diameter 31 cm (12⅛ in),

commercial product

Cover from Soleil du Dimanche, 1897

Colour lithograph, 40 x 29 cm (15¾ x 11⅜ in),

magazine cover

The Flowers: Iris, 1898

Colour lithograph, 103.5 x 43.3 cm (40¾ x 17 in),
decorative panel

The Arts: Poetry, 1898

Colour lithograph, 60 x 38 cm (23⅝ x 15 in),
decorative panel

Alphonse Mucha

MAKE YOUR OWN ART MASTERPIECE

The Moon and the Stars:
The Moon, 1902

Colour lithograph, 56 x 21 cm (22 x 8⅛ in),
decorative panel

Alphonse Mucha
MAKE YOUR OWN ART MASTERPIECE

The Seasons: Summer, 1896

Colour lithograph, 28 x 14.5 cm (11 x 5¾ in),
decorative panel

Alphonse Mucha

MAKE YOUR OWN ART MASTERPIECE

Dusk, 1899

Colour lithograph, 68 x 103 cm (26¾ x 40½ in),
decorative panel

Alphonse Mucha
MAKE YOUR OWN ART MASTERPIECE

Woman with a Daisy, 1900

Colour lithograph, 65 x 83 cm (25½ x 32⅝ in),
decorative panel

Alphonse Mucha

MAKE YOUR OWN ART MASTERPIECE

Reverie, 1897

Colour lithograph, 72.7 x 55.2 cm (28⅝ x 21¾ in),
decorative panel

Laurel, 1901

Colour lithograph, 53 x 39.5 cm (20$\frac{7}{8}$ x 15$\frac{1}{2}$ in),
decorative panel

Zodiac, 1896

Colour lithograph, 65.7 x 48.2 cm (26 x 19 in),
decorative panel

Monaco Monte Carlo, 1897

Colour lithograph, 108 x 74.5 cm (42½ x 29¼ in),
commercial poster

Alphonse Mucha

MAKE YOUR OWN ART MASTERPIECE

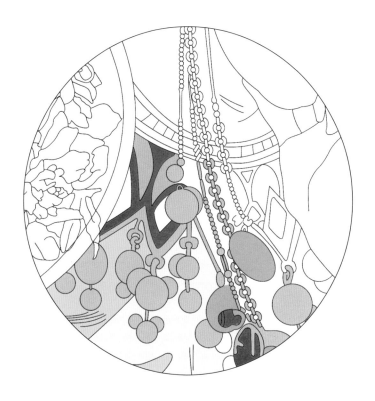

Byzantine, *1900*

Colour lithograph, approx. 53 x 39.5 cm (20⅞ x 15½ in),
decorative panel

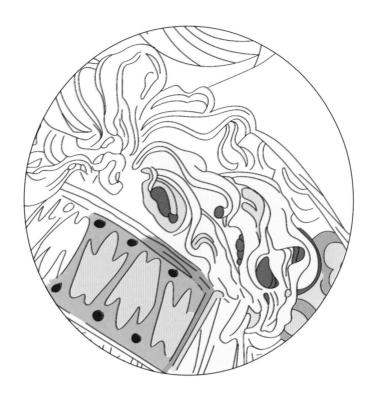

Langage des Fleurs, 1900

Colour lithograph, 26.4 x 36.2 cm (10⅖ x 14¼ in),
decorative panel

Alphonse Mucha

**The Times of the Day: Evening
Contemplation,** 1899

Colour lithograph, 107.7 x 39 cm (42⅜ x 15¼ in),
decorative panel

The Flowers: Lily, 1898

Colour lithograph, 103.5 x 43.3 cm (40¾ x 17 in),
decorative panel

Alphonse Mucha
MAKE YOUR OWN ART MASTERPIECE

Ivy, 1901

Colour lithograph, 53 x 39.5 cm (20⅞ x 15½ in),
decorative panel

For further illustrated books on a wide range of

art subjects, in various formats, please look at our website:

www.flametreepublishing.com